# Making a House

by Rebecca Weber

A pencil is a tool.
I will make the plan
with it.

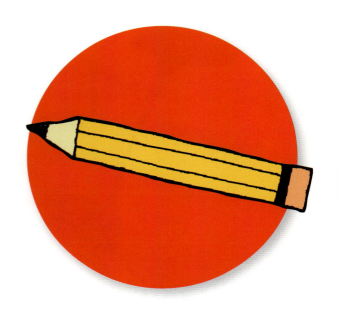

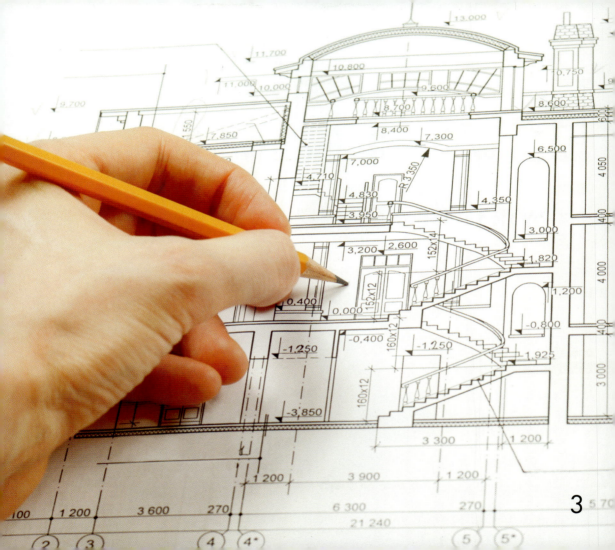

A saw is a tool.
I will cut the wood
with it.

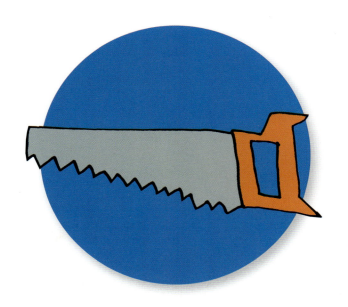

5

A hammer is a tool.
I will hit the nail
with it.

# A ruler is a tool.

A drill is a tool, too.

A paintbrush is a tool.
I will paint the wall
with it.

A broom is a tool.
I will sweep the floor
with it.

A truck is a tool.
I will move into
the house with it.

I move into the house!